on toast

on toast

Susannah Blake   *photography by* William Lingwood

RYLAND
PETERS
& SMALL

LONDON NEW YORK

Senior Designer Paul Tilby
Commissioning Editor Elsa Petersen-Schepelern
Editor Susan Stuck
Production Sheila Smith

Art Director Gabriella Le Grazie
Publishing Director Alison Starling

Food Stylist Jenny White
Prop Stylist Antonia Gaunt

DEDICATION

For Sheila, because Brussels sprouts should never go on toast.

NOTES

- All spoon measurements are level unless otherwise stated.

- Eggs are large unless otherwise specified. Uncooked or partially cooked eggs should not be served to the very old, frail, young children, pregnant women, or those with compromised immune systems.

First published in the USA by
Ryland Peters & Small, Inc.
519 Broadway, 5th Floor
New York, NY 10012
www.rylandpeters.com

10 9 8 7 6 5 4 3 2 1

Text © Susannah Blake 2005
Design and photographs ©
Ryland Peters & Small 2005

Library of Congress
Cataloging-in-Publication Data

Blake, Susannah.
 On toast / Susannah Blake ;
photography by William Lingwood.
    p. cm.
 Includes index.
 ISBN 1-84172-956-6
 1. Cookery (Bread) I. Title.

 TX769.B59 2005
 641.8'15--dc22

                        2005000653

Printed in China

contents

crisp comfort

From the tiniest, crispest, most garlicky bruschetta topped with fresh tomatoes and sprinkled with olive oil to the thickest, most delicious toast slathered in butter and jam, there's something about toast that is instantly appealing, utterly pleasing, and immensely satisfying. The aroma of cooking toast—whether it's in a toaster, under the broiler, or on a stovetop grill-pan—is almost as enticing as the smell of fresh baked bread, and it seems to conjure up the same emotions. When you smell toast, you just want to eat it.

Toast doesn't just have to mean a slice of bread cooked on both sides until golden. The options are many, and always delicious. In these pages you'll find small, biteable crostini, crisp bruschetta, wedges of toasted rye, slabs of broiled sourdough, sautéed French toast, pan-grilled focaccia, and toasted ciabatta—all forming the base of the most delicious, indulgent feasts. Whatever you're toasting though, you should top it and eat it immediately, while it's still warm and crisp.

Although certain breads are suggested for each recipe, feel free to mix and match and experiment with whatever other breads are available. If you find a fabulous bread at a speciality bakery, it's almost guaranteed to be delicious toasted, so try it in a recipe that uses a similar bread. Slender fingers of ciabatta can be just as good used instead of richly flavored focaccia, and slices of fruit bread can be just as tempting as Italian panettone. Whole wheat breads can be used instead of white and vice versa. Just go with your own taste and above all—enjoy. Toast is always irresistible, so it's hard to go wrong.

melting cheese and ham croissants

1 teaspoon wholegrain mustard

1 teaspoon balsamic vinegar

1 tablespoon olive oil

2 slices of prosciutto
or other wafer-thin cured ham,
about 1 oz.

½ ripe peach

2 croissants

2 large slices of Swiss cheese,
such as Gruyère or Emmental,
about 2 oz.

Serves 2

Great for breakfast, but just as good for brunch, lunch, a mid-afternoon snack or midnight feast, this winning combination of toasted croissant, melting Gruyère, wafer-thin slices of ham and juicy fresh peaches can't be beaten. It's good made with wedges of fresh fig too.

Put the mustard, vinegar, and oil in a bowl, mix well, then set aside. Cut the ham slices in half lengthwise to make 4 long strips. Slice the peach into thin wedges. Preheat the broiler.

Split the croissants in half and arrange on the broiler pan, cut side down. Cook for about 2 minutes until very lightly toasted, then flip over and fold a slice of cheese on the bottom half of each one. Cook until the cheese is melting, and the top halves are golden. (The top halves will be done just before the cheese-covered halves, so remove and keep them warm.)

Arrange the ham and peach wedges over the melting cheese, drizzle over the dressing, top with the second half of the croissant, and serve immediately.

breakfast
toast

toasted bagels

with cream cheese
and smoked salmon

2 bagels

½ cup cream cheese

4 oz. sliced smoked salmon

lemon wedges,
for squeezing

freshly ground
black pepper

Serves 2

You can't mess about with a classic like this because the old way is still the best. All you need is warm bagels toasted until just crisp, then slathered with creamy cheese, layers of smoked salmon, and a good squeeze of lemon juice.

Split the bagels in half horizontally and toast on both sides in a toaster, under the broiler, or using a stovetop grill-pan.

Spread the bottom half of each bagel with cream cheese and fold the slices of smoked salmon on top. Squeeze over plenty of lemon juice, sprinkle with black pepper, and serve topped with the second half of the bagel.

eggs florentine on toasted english muffins

2 eggs

1 tablespoon butter, plus extra for spreading

8 oz. baby spinach leaves

a pinch of freshly grated nutmeg

2 English muffins

2–4 tablespoons hollandaise sauce

sea salt and freshly ground black pepper

Serves 2

You can buy excellent ready-made hollandaise sauce in large supermarkets, taking all the hassle out of making this divine breakfast. If you can't find hollandaise, a good-quality cheese sauce works just as well.

Half-fill a saucepan with boiling water and bring to a boil. Reduce the heat to a gentle simmer, then crack each egg into a cup and gently slide into the water. Cook for about 4 minutes until firm, then remove with a slotted spoon and drain well on paper towels.

Meanwhile, melt the butter in a saucepan, then add the spinach. Cook for about 3 minutes, stirring occasionally, until the spinach begins to wilt. Season with nutmeg, salt, and pepper, remove from the heat, cover, and keep it warm.

Split the muffins, toast on both sides, and spread with butter. Spoon the spinach onto the bottom half of each muffin (taking care to drain off any excess liquid as you do so). Set an egg on top of each mound of spinach, spoon over the hollandaise sauce, sprinkle with a little more black pepper, and serve immediately.

creamy scrambled eggs on rye
with cinnamon-honey roasted tomatoes

Perfect for a leisurely breakfast or brunch when you've got time to sit back and relax. Add a drizzle of honey and a pinch of cinnamon to the tomatoes and you give them an irresistibly warm, scented sweetness that goes perfectly with the smooth, creamy eggs and earthy, pungent rye.

3 plum tomatoes

¼ teaspoon ground cinnamon

1 teaspoon honey

½ tablespoon olive oil

4 eggs

1 tablespoon heavy cream

4 slices of light rye bread

2 tablespoons butter, plus extra for spreading

sea salt and freshly ground black pepper

Serves 2

Cut the tomatoes in half lengthwise and arrange in a baking dish, cut side up. Sprinkle with cinnamon, salt, and pepper and drizzle over the honey and olive oil. Roast in a preheated oven at 425°F for 30 minutes, pouring any juices back over the tomatoes part way through cooking.

When the tomatoes are nearly cooked, put the eggs and cream in a bowl, season with salt and pepper, and beat briefly. Toast the rye bread in a toaster or under the broiler and keep it warm.

Melt the butter in a small, nonstick saucepan over medium-low heat until sizzling. Pour in the eggs and cook gently for 1–2 minutes, stirring constantly, until thick and creamy. (The eggs will continue to cook after you remove the pan from the heat, so be careful not to overcook.)

Quickly butter the rye toast and put 2 slices on each plate. Spoon the scrambled eggs on top and pile 3 tomato halves on each serving. Spoon over any extra tomato juices, sprinkle with black pepper, and serve immediately.

Note Don't use dark, moist rye bread such as pumpernickel for this recipe. It doesn't toast well, and won't give the delicious crispness of a light rye.

toasted brioche
with lemon cream and fresh raspberries

This incredibly quick and easy breakfast is the ultimate in no-fuss indulgence. For best results, choose a really good-quality lemon curd with a fresh, zingy flavor, and a thick, mild-tasting yogurt. It's a good idea to check the flavor of the lemon cream once you've mixed it up—if you use a bland lemon curd, you may have to add a little extra.

Put the sour cream, yogurt, and lemon curd in a bowl and mix briefly. Set aside.

Cut the brioche buns in half and lightly toast under a preheated broiler. Arrange the base of each brioche on a plate, spoon the lemon cream mixture on top, then pile on the raspberries. Add the toasted lid, dust with confectioners' sugar, if using, and serve immediately.

Note If brioche buns aren't available, use thick slices of toasted brioche instead.

½ cup sour cream, crème fraîche, or heavy cream

½ cup plain yogurt

3–4 tablespoons lemon curd

3–4 individual brioche buns

1½ cups fresh raspberries, 6–8 oz.

confectioners' sugar, to dust (optional)

Serves 3–4

marinated red onions and anchovies on focaccia fingers

Aromatic sweet-and-sour onions are the perfect foil for salty, pungent anchovies, while lightly broiled, puffy, dimpled focaccia flavored with olive oil makes an ideal base. In Liguria, focaccia's birthplace, the bread is baked in huge rectangles and you can buy it in square slabs, as well as in round or freeform loaves.

1½ red onions, halved and thinly sliced

2 teaspoons sugar

¼ teaspoon salt

½ cup white wine vinegar

1 teaspoon juniper berries, lightly crushed

2 tablespoons chopped fresh dill, plus extra to serve

a slab of focaccia, about 10 x 3 inches

6 anchovies, halved lengthwise

Makes 12

Put the sliced onion in a bowl, cover with boiling water, then drain immediately. Drain well, tip into a bowl, and separate the layers with your fingers.

Put the sugar, salt, and vinegar in a separate bowl and stir until dissolved, then add the juniper berries. Sprinkle the dill over the onions, add the vinegar mixture, and stir well. Let stand for 1 hour, stirring once or twice.

When ready to serve, drain the onions well. Preheat a ridged stovetop grill-pan. Split the focaccia in half horizontally, then slice each half into 6 fingers and press down onto the pan. Toast for about 3 minutes until well marked, then flip over and toast the second side. Pile the onions on the toasts and top each one with a strip of anchovy.

bitesize
toast

grilled zucchini and feta on crisp ciabatta
with minty lemon dressing

These salty, minty, zesty toasts make a perfect alfresco snack to serve on a balmy summer evening with a glass of chilled white wine. Use small, firm zucchini; they have a much sweeter flavor and better texture than the larger, spongy ones available later in the season.

To make the dressing, put the mint, lemon juice, lemon zest, and oil in a bowl, add a little salt and plenty of pepper, and whisk well. Set aside.

Cut each zucchini lengthwise into 4 slices and brush both sides with oil. Heat a stovetop grill-pan until very hot, then press a few of the zucchini slices onto the pan and cook for about 3 minutes until well marked. Flip over and cook for another 2–3 minutes until tender. Lift the slices out of the pan, roll up loosely, and keep them warm while you cook the remaining slices.

Split the ciabatta in half horizontally, then cut each half into 6 pieces. Toast the slices on both sides under a preheated broiler until golden. Whisk the dressing again, then dip in a slice of zucchini, and fold it onto a piece of toast. Crumble over some feta cheese and sprinkle with a little extra dressing. Repeat with the remaining toasts and serve.

3 zucchini, about 1 lb.

olive oil, for brushing

1 ciabatta loaf

4 oz. feta cheese

Minty lemon dressing

1 tablespoon finely chopped fresh mint

1 tablespoon lemon juice

½ teaspoon freshly grated unwaxed lemon zest

3 tablespoons olive oil

sea salt and freshly ground black pepper

Makes 12

caramelized shallots on parmesan toasts

3 oz. Parmesan cheese, in one piece

2 tablespoons butter, at room temperature

1 small or medium baguette

Caramelized shallots

1 tablespoon butter, at room temperature

1 cup thinly sliced shallots, about 8 oz.

½ tablespoon sugar

3 tablespoons sherry

2 sprigs of thyme, plus extra to serve

sea salt and freshly ground black pepper

Sweet, meltingly tender shallots transform this cheese on toast into something utterly sublime. They're also delicious spread on a plain toasted baguette or chunky country-style toast that has been smeared thickly with Gorgonzola, then lightly broiled.

To cook the shallots, melt the butter in a nonstick skillet over gentle heat. Add the shallots, sprinkle with a little salt, and cook, stirring, for 5–10 minutes until translucent and golden. Sprinkle with the sugar and continue cooking for about 5 minutes until the sugar begins to caramelize. Pour over the sherry, add the thyme, and cook gently for about 10 minutes until the shallots are tender. Increase the heat and bubble vigorously until all the liquid has evaporated. Add salt and pepper to taste. Remove from the heat and cover to keep warm.

Grate half the Parmesan and pare the rest into shavings using a vegetable peeler. Put the butter in a bowl, add the grated Parmesan and mix well.

Slice the baguette. Put some of the Parmesan butter on each one, then top with the Parmesan shavings. Toast under a preheated broiler for about 3 minutes until golden and bubbling. Spoon the caramelized shallots on top, add extra thyme, if using, and serve.

Makes 8–12

crostini

topped with blue cheese and caramelized pear

These crispy, crunchy little toasts are great for serving with drinks. The warm, sweet pear goes perfectly with the pungent blue cheese and slightly fragrant flavor of the pecans (although they are just as good with cheese and pear alone).

Cut the baguette diagonally into 12 thin slices, just under ½ inch thick. Brush with oil, then toast on both sides until crisp and golden. Let cool.

Melt the butter in a nonstick skillet, add the pears, and cook for 10 minutes, turning occasionally until golden and caramelized. Remove the pears from the pan, then top each crostini with a thin slice of Gorgonzola, a wedge of pear, and a pecan half, if using.

Note The pears are boiling hot when they come out of the pan, so leave for a couple of minutes before serving to give them time to cool down.

½ thin baguette

olive oil, for brushing

2 tablespoons butter

1 pear, halved, peeled, cored, and cut into 12 thin wedges

4 oz. Gorgonzola or other blue cheese

12 pecan halves (optional)

Makes 12

beets and sour cream on crunchy rye

These little toasts have a hint of eastern Europe about them. They're particularly good served with ice-cold shots of vodka—making them the perfect party nibble.

8 oz. cooked beets

1 teaspoon balsamic vinegar

1 teaspoon wholegrain mustard

2 tablespoons olive oil

3 slices of light rye bread

⅓ cup sour cream

Makes 12

Cut the beets into ¼ inch slices, then cut in the opposite direction to make thin matchsticks. Put in a bowl.

Put the vinegar, mustard, and oil in another bowl, whisk well, then pour it over the beets and toss gently, making sure they are well coated.

Cut each slice of bread into fourths and toast on both sides under a preheated broiler or on a ridged stovetop grill-pan. Arrange on a plate, add a dollop of sour cream to each piece of toast, then put some sliced beets on top and serve.

Note If buying ready-cooked beets, be sure that they haven't been preserved in vinegar. You need plain cooked beets; the pickled variety will give unpleasant results.

melting cheese and sun-dried tomatoes on toast

1 tablespoon olive oil

1 shallot, finely chopped

2 tablespoons white wine

½ cup grated Cheddar or similar sharp cheese

½ teaspoon cornstarch, mixed with 1 teaspoon water

2 thick slices of white bread

½ garlic clove

2 sun-dried tomatoes in olive oil, cut into thin strips

2 sprigs of fresh oregano

hot red pepper flakes, for sprinkling

Inspired by the classic Welsh rabbit, this substantial snack is sure to keep hunger pangs at bay. Enjoy big, manly slabs of toast, or cut the bread into delicate fingers before toasting and topping with the cheese mixture.

Heat the oil in a small skillet and add the shallot. Sauté gently for about 5 minutes until translucent. Stir in the wine and cheese, then the cornstarch mixture. Heat gently, stirring, until the cheese has melted and the mixture is creamy.

Meanwhile, toast the bread on one side. Turn it over, rub with the cut side of the garlic, pour over the cheese, and broil until golden and bubbling. Remove from the heat and top with the strips of sun-dried tomato, oregano, and a sprinkling of hot red pepper flakes.

Serves 2

snack toast

tomato, basil, and mozzarella bruschetta

8 oz. grape or cherry tomatoes, halved

1–1½ handfuls of fresh basil leaves, torn

3 tablespoons olive oil, plus extra for drizzling (optional)

12 slices of ciabatta, about 1 inch thick

1 garlic clove, halved

1 mozzarella cheese, about 6 oz., torn into bite-size pieces (buffalo mozzarella is best)

sea salt and freshly ground black pepper

Serves 4: makes 12

These wonderful, juicy toasts make a perfect snack or informal appetizer to serve with drinks. They're great just with tomatoes and basil, but even better with a chunk of chewy, mild mozzarella on top. Ciabatta is used here, but any sourdough bread will do.

Put the tomatoes and basil in a bowl. Spoon over the olive oil, season well with salt and pepper, and toss lightly. Set aside for about 15 minutes.

When ready to serve, toast the ciabatta slices on both sides under a preheated broiler until crisp and golden. Rub the cut side of the garlic on each piece of toast, then spoon the tomato and basil mixture on top. Add a piece of mozzarella to each one, spoon over the juices remaining in the bowl, and sprinkle with extra oil, if using. Grind a little more black pepper on top and serve.

mushrooms on toast

Another treat that's good at any time of day, these juicy, fragrant mushrooms are really rich and garlicky. Pile them up on thick slices of hot buttered whole-wheat toast or crusty, country-style sourdough—and if you're feeling really indulgent, add a spoonful of creamy mascarpone.

1 tablespoon olive oil

2 shallots, finely sliced

1 garlic clove, finely chopped

6 oz. button mushrooms

¼ cup white wine

1 sprig of thyme,
plus extra to serve (optional)

2 thick slices of whole-wheat bread
or country-style sourdough

butter, for spreading

sea salt and freshly
ground black pepper

Heat the oil in a skillet, add the shallots, and sauté gently for 2 minutes, then add the garlic and cook for a further minute.

Add the mushrooms, toss to coat in the garlicky oil, then add the white wine, thyme, and a pinch of salt. Increase the heat and bring to a boil, then bubble gently for about 10 minutes until the mushrooms are tender and the juices have been absorbed.

When the mushrooms are nearly cooked, toast the bread on both sides and spread with the butter. Season the mushrooms with black pepper, check if they need any more salt, then pile on the toast. Top with fresh thyme, if using, and serve.

Serves 2

spiced halibut and red onions on toasted focaccia

Strips of delicately flavored halibut are delicious rolled in crushed spices and piled on top of moist, chewy focaccia—but you can use any firm-fleshed white fish. Sardine fillets are good cooked this way too. If you can find focaccia flavored with sun-dried tomatoes, try it—it's particularly good under the spicy, lemony fish.

Toast the cumin and coriander seeds and red pepper flakes in a dry skillet for about 1 minute until aromatic, then grind coarsely with a mortar and pestle. Tip onto a plate, then add salt and pepper.

Slice the fish into ½-inch strips. Put the lemon juice in a dish, dip the strips in the juice, then put on the plate of spices and roll to cover, rubbing the spices all over. Leaving the root intact, slice the onion into about 8 wedges and nestle them around the fish. Sprinkle with more lemon juice and let stand for about 10 minutes.

When you are ready to cook the fish, preheat the broiler. Split the focaccia in half to make 2 large, thin slices and toast both sides until crisp and golden.

Meanwhile, heat the oil in a nonstick skillet and add the onion. Sauté for 2 minutes, then flip over and add the fish to the pan. Cook for about 1 minute on each side until cooked through, then arrange the onion and fish on the toasts and serve immediately.

¼ teaspoon cumin seeds

1 teaspoon coriander seeds

2 good pinches of hot red pepper flakes

4 oz. skinned halibut fillet

freshly squeezed juice of ½ lemon

½ red onion

1 slice of focaccia, about 4 x 3 inches

4 teaspoons olive oil

sea salt and freshly ground black pepper

Serves 2

panzanella toasts

Inspired by panzanella, the classic Tuscan bread salad, in this recipe the bread is under the salad rather than in it. Rich with the flavors of basil, capers, and garlic, the tangy juices and dressing still soak into the toast creating an utterly wonderful, oozingly juicy snack. Choose the juiciest, ripest, best-flavored tomatoes.

1 red bell pepper

1 yellow bell pepper

4 ripe tomatoes

4 anchovies, halved lengthwise

1 tablespoon salted capers, rinsed and coarsely chopped

½ garlic clove, minced

½ tablespoon red wine vinegar

2 tablespoons olive oil

a handful of fresh basil leaves, torn

2 large slices of rustic sourdough bread, or ½ loaf ciabatta, split in half

freshly ground black pepper

Serves 2

Preheat the oven to 450°F. Put the bell peppers on a baking tray and cook for about 30 minutes until charred. Remove from the oven, put in a plastic bag, and let cool for about 10 minutes.

Meanwhile, cut a cross in the base of each tomato, put in a bowl, and cover with boiling water. Let stand for about 30 seconds, then drain and peel. Halve the tomatoes, remove the tough core, and scoop the seeds into a strainer set over a bowl. Press out any juice from the seeds and discard the seeds. Tear up the tomato flesh and put in another bowl. Add the anchovies.

Remove the blackened skin from the bell peppers (do not wash the peeled peppers or you will lose the smoky flavor), then discard the stem, core, and seeds. Chop or tear the flesh and add to the tomatoes.

Add the capers, garlic, vinegar, olive oil, and torn basil to the reserved tomato juices. Add a good grinding of black pepper and whisk well. Pour over the salad, toss gently, then let stand for about 20 minutes to develop the flavors.

To serve, toast the bread on both sides on a hot stovetop grill-pan or under a preheated broiler, then pile the salad on top, spooning over the juices.

fresh fig and goat cheese on walnut toast

Pungent, salty goat cheese goes particularly well with the subtly sweet flavors of fig and honey. Look for small, firm whole goat cheeses that you can slice easily, and try to find a flat, round loaf of walnut bread to make long, elegant toasts.

Toast the walnut bread on one side under a preheated broiler. Turn over and top each slice with 2 slices of goat cheese. Drizzle ½ teaspoon honey over each one and broil for about 5 minutes until golden and bubbling. (Set a dish under the broiler to catch any honey that dribbles off the toast.)

Arrange the toasts on a plate, pour any honey from the dish back over the toasts, and sprinkle with the pine nuts. Using a teaspoon, scoop the pink flesh from the fig and spoon over the goat cheese. Serve immediately.

Note To toast the pine nuts, toss them in a dry, nonstick pan over medium heat until golden brown all over. Be careful not to let them burn.

2 thin slices of walnut bread

4 thin slices of goat cheese, about 3 oz.

1 teaspoon honey

1 tablespoon toasted pine nuts

1 fresh fig, halved

Serves 2

rare beef baguette
with fresh mango salsa

The great thing about good-quality beef is that it tastes fabulous just seared on a stovetop grill-pan until pink and juicy. The fiery green wasabi adds a lively bite to the sweet, aromatic salsa—so add as much or as little as you like.

about 8 oz. steak

olive oil, for brushing

½ baguette

Fresh mango salsa

½ large mango

2 tablespoons chopped cilantro

freshly squeezed juice of ½ lime

¼–½ teaspoon wasabi paste

sea salt

aluminum foil

To make the salsa, peel the mango, chop the flesh, and put in a bowl. Sprinkle with the chopped cilantro.

Mix the lime juice and wasabi paste in a separate bowl and season with a little salt. Pour over the mango and herbs and toss gently. Set aside.

Trim off any fat or sinew from the meat and brush with olive oil. Heat a stovetop grill-pan until very hot, brush with more oil, then press the meat down on it for about 2 minutes. Flip over and cook for a further 2 minutes, then cook for a further 2 minutes on each side, or until cooked to your taste. Lift onto a board, cover with foil, and let rest for 10 minutes.

When you're nearly ready to serve, split the baguette in half and toast the cut side under a preheated broiler until golden. Slice the meat thinly and arrange on top of the baguette. Add the mango salsa, spoon over any meat juices, and serve immediately.

Serves 2

big toast

grilled chicken and avocado baguette
with tarragon mayo

This giant wedge of toast is a meal in itself and is sure to satisfy even the most ravenous appetite. Each mouthful offers an explosion of flavors and textures with the zesty, zingy, tangy mayo oozing out around the juicy chicken, smooth buttery avocado, and sweet tomatoes. It's messy to eat, so you might need a napkin or two.

Cut the chicken diagonally into ½-inch strips. Put the mustard, honey, lemon juice, and oil in a bowl with a good sprinkling of salt and pepper, then mix well. Add the chicken and toss to coat. Set aside for 10 minutes.

Meanwhile, put the mayonnaise, lemon zest and juice, and herbs in a bowl and mix well. Season with a little pepper, then set aside.

Cut the tomatoes in half lengthwise, then cut the avocado in half and remove the pit and skin. Cut the flesh into large chunks.

Heat a stovetop grill-pan until very hot, brush with oil, and spread out the chicken strips on it. Cook for about 2 minutes, then flip over and cook for 1 minute more until cooked through. Remove from the pan and keep them warm.

Cut the baguette in half lengthwise and toast the cut side under a preheated broiler. Spread the baguette halves with the mayonnaise, then arrange the chicken, tomatoes, and avocado on top. Sprinkle with extra pepper to taste and serve immediately.

2 skinless, boneless chicken breasts

1 teaspoon Dijon mustard

1 teaspoon honey

2 teaspoons lemon juice

1 tablespoon olive oil, plus extra for brushing

8–10 cherry tomatoes

1 small, perfectly ripe avocado

1 medium baguette, about 10 inches long

sea salt and freshly ground black pepper

Tarragon mayonnaise

¼ cup homemade or good-quality storebought mayonnaise

freshly grated zest of ½ unwaxed lemon

2 teaspoons lemon juice

2 tablespoons chopped fresh tarragon

Serves 2

giant prosciutto, brie, and tomato toasts
with fresh arugula

10–12 grape or cherry tomatoes

1 teaspoon balsamic vinegar

1 tablespoon olive oil

1 ciabatta loaf

4 slices proscuitto or thinly sliced smoked ham

6 oz. Brie cheese

2 handfuls of arugula

freshly ground black pepper

Serves 2

This mammoth, melting toast is the closest thing to an instant pizza that you could wish for—with the juicy tomatoes and arugula adding a wonderful fresh zing. Try to find very sweet, juicy, well-flavored tomatoes— the vine-ripened ones are particularly good.

Cut the tomatoes in half and put in a bowl. Sprinkle with the vinegar and olive oil, season with pepper, and toss gently. Set aside.

Split the ciabatta in half and set under a preheated broiler, cut side down. Toast until crisp and golden. Meanwhile, cut each slice of prosciutto into 3 pieces.

Turn the bread over and arrange the strips of prosciutto and slices of Brie on the uncooked side. Broil for a further 5 minutes or so until the bread is golden, the ham crisp, and the cheese golden and bubbling.

Spoon the tomatoes on top, sprinkle with any extra dressing, top each toast with a handful of arugula, and serve immediately.

spicy sautéed potatoes and chorizo on toast

This manly feast is not for the faint-hearted and is perfect when you get in late after a night out. The crisp, golden potatoes absorb the flavors of the chorizo, and the rich, spicy, garlicky oil is just delicious when it soaks into the toast. If you like things extra hot, feel free to sprinkle with a little more red pepper flakes.

Heat the oil in a large skillet until hot, add the potatoes, and sauté for about 5 minutes. Add the chorizo and continue sautéing, turning occasionally, until the potatoes are crisp and golden. Sprinkle with the garlic and pepper flakes and sauté for a further 2 minutes.

Meanwhile, toast the bread on both sides under a preheated broiler, on a stovetop grill-pan, or in the toaster. Spoon the potato and chorizo mixture on top, drizzling over any extra oil from the pan, then serve. (Be careful, because the potatoes will be hot.)

3 tablespoons olive oil

6 oz. new potatoes, boiled and cut into bite-size chunks

4 oz. chorizo sausage, cut into bite-size chunks

1 garlic clove, crushed

½ teaspoon hot red pepper flakes

4 slices of country-style sourdough bread

sea salt and freshly ground black pepper

Serves 2

tuna melt

6 oz. canned tuna, drained

3–3½ tablespoons homemade or good-quality store-bought mayonnaise

½ tablespoon capers, rinsed and finely chopped

2 gherkins or 1 dill pickle in sweet vinegar, diced fairly finely, plus extra to serve

¼ red bell pepper, chopped fairly finely

1 tablespoon chopped fresh tarragon

2 large, thick slices of white crusty bread

4 large, thin slices Swiss cheese, such as Gruyère or Emmenthal

freshly ground black pepper

Serves 2

The first tuna melt I ever came across was in New York. It was a towering, melting extravaganza—but alas, it wasn't my order and it went to the next table. I have been striving to create the ultimate tuna melt ever since—and I think this might be it. Use any kind of white bread—crusty rustic sourdough, a large French country loaf, a freshly baked sandwich loaf— just make sure the slices are large and thick.

Put the tuna in a bowl and flake the flesh. Add the mayonnaise, capers, gherkins, peppers, and tarragon and mix well. Season with plenty of pepper.

Toast the bread on one side under a preheated broiler, then turn it over and spread the tuna thickly on the uncooked side. Put 2 cheese slices on top of each toast and broil for about 5 minutes until the cheese is golden and bubbling. Serve with extra pickles.

Note Look for tuna canned in water rather than brine— the capers are salty enough already.

butternut squash and blue cheese giant toasts

Sweet, melting, roasted squash and tangy blue cheese are the most sublime combination—on chunky toast, they're even better. Choose a really gooey cheese that's going to melt instantly with the heat of the squash and ooze over the toast.

Scoop the seeds out of the squash and cut the flesh lengthwise into 4 wedges. Put in a baking dish, brush with olive oil, and sprinkle with salt and pepper. Roast in a preheated oven at 400°F for 45 minutes until tender, then remove from the oven and let cool slightly. When the squash is cool enough to handle, cut away the skin and discard.

To make the dressing, whisk the vinegar and oil in a bowl and set aside.

Toast the bread on one side under a preheated broiler, then turn it over. Arrange the squash on the untoasted side, put slices of the cheese on top, and broil until the cheese is bubbling and the bread golden. Top each one with a handful of spinach leaves, pour over a few spoonfuls of the dressing, and serve.

½ small butternut squash, about 10 oz.

olive oil, for brushing

2 large, thick slices of rustic sourdough bread, or 4 smaller slices

3 oz. blue cheese, such as Gorgonzola or dolcelatte

a handful of baby spinach leaves

sea salt and freshly ground black pepper

Dressing

½ tablespoon balsamic vinegar

1 tablespoon olive oil

Serves 2

¼ cup light cream

2 egg yolks

freshly grated zest
of ½ unwaxed orange

2 teaspoons freshly
squeezed orange juice

1 teaspoon sugar

1 tablespoon butter

2 thick slices of panettone,
cut in half

icing sugar, to dust

orange zest, to decorate

creamy orange french toast

This unbelievably delicious French toast is a divine concoction. It's a perfect treat in winter when panettone, the traditional Italian Christmas bread, is widely available.

Orange cream

3 tablespoons sour cream
or heavy cream

1 teaspoon
confectioners' sugar

1 tablespoon orange juice

½ teaspoon lemon juice

Serves 2

To make the orange cream, put the sour cream, sugar, and orange and lemon juices in a bowl and stir until smooth and creamy. Set aside.

Put the light cream, egg yolks, orange zest and juice, and sugar in a wide, shallow dish and beat well. Heat the butter in a large, nonstick skillet. Dip each slice of panettone in the custard mixture, coating each side well, then carefully arrange in the skillet. Spoon any remaining custard mixture over the toasts, and sauté for about 2 minutes until golden underneath.

Very carefully, flip the toasts over and cook for a further 1–2 minutes until golden. Put 2 slices of French toast on each plate, then dust with confectioners' sugar, drizzle over the orange cream, and top with strips of orange zest.

indulgent toast

sticky sautéed bananas on toast

4 tablespoons butter,
plus extra for spreading

3 perfectly ripe bananas, sliced

2 tablespoons brown sugar

1 tablespoon brandy

½ lime

2 thick slices of challah or white bread

heavy cream or vanilla ice cream, to serve

Serves 2

One mouthful of these buttery, sticky, gooey, tangy bananas will transport you to another world—just be careful about putting too much in your mouth in one go because those bananas are HOT when they first come out of the pan! Challah, the delicious, dense Jewish bread, makes the perfect base, but any good-quality white bread will be divine.

Melt the butter in a nonstick skillet until sizzling, then add the bananas and sauté for about 2 minutes. Turn them over, sprinkle with the brown sugar, and continue cooking for a further 2–3 minutes, gently nudging the bananas around the skillet, but taking care not to break them up.

Add the brandy and cook for 1 minute more until the bananas are soft and tender, letting the juices bubble. Remove the pan from the heat, squeeze over the lime juice, and shake the bananas to mix.

Meanwhile, lightly toast the bread on both sides, add the bananas, and top with cream or a generous scoop of vanilla ice cream. Serve immediately.

macerated berries on brioche french toast

This luscious toast is something like an indulgent trifle, with the sweet, alcoholic juices soaking into the brioche and the rich, creamy mascarpone sliding off the top. You can use any combination of summer berries, but I like strawberries and blueberries the best.

Cut the strawberries in half, if large, and put in a bowl with the blueberries. Sprinkle with the sugar, then add the Grand Marnier and let macerate for at least 1 hour.

Just before serving, put the mascarpone and confectioners' sugar in a bowl and stir in 2–3 teaspoons of the macerating juices from the berries.

Lightly toast the brioche on both sides, then spread with a thick layer of mascarpone and spoon the macerated berries and all the juices on top. Top with fresh mint leaves, if using, and serve.

1 cup strawberries, hulled, about 4 oz.

⅓ cup blueberries, about 2 oz.

1 teaspoon sugar

2½ tablespoons Grand Marnier

3 tablespoons mascarpone cheese

1 tablespoon confectioners' sugar

2 thick slices of brioche

fresh mint leaves, to serve (optional)

Serves 2

armagnac-soaked prunes on toasted almond croissants

If you thought you couldn't beat a classic prune and Armagnac tart, just wait until you've tried this toast. For a taste of pure heaven, look out for really moist almond croissants with a good thick layer of soft, sticky almond paste. (Don't forget you have to let the prunes soak, so be sure to leave enough time!)

1 cup pitted prunes, about 20

½ cup boiling water

2 tablespoons Armagnac

2 almond croissants

heavy cream, to serve

Serves 2

Put the prunes in a bowl and add the boiling water. Cover and let soak for at least 1½ hours.

Tip the prunes and soaking juices into a saucepan and bring to a boil. Simmer for 5 minutes until the juices are syrupy, then add the brandy and bubble for a few seconds longer.

Meanwhile, carefully split each almond croissant in half to make 2 flat crescents. Broil the cut sides until golden and crisp around the edges, then pile the prunes on top and spoon over the juices and the cream. Serve immediately.

nutty chocolate and marshmallow toast

Sinfully sweet and sticky, this toast is the ultimate in instant comfort food. It's lacking sophistication by anyone's standards— but it makes a luscious treat when you're feeling blue and need a no-effort pick-me-up.

Toast the bread on one side under a preheated broiler, then flip over. Pour the cream over the untoasted side, sprinkle with the grated or shaved chocolate, nuts, and marshmallows, and broil until golden and bubbling. Eat with caution: the topping will be hot!

Note This is definitely a recipe for those with a sweet tooth. You can use any type of white bread—a classic square white loaf, a French country loaf, or several slices of white baguette cut on the diagonal. However, don't be tempted to try it with a sweet bread such as brioche or panettone—there's only so much sugar you should eat at once!

2 thick slices of white bread

2 tablespoons light cream

½ oz. semisweet chocolate, grated or shaved, or good quality chocolate chips

a handful of pecans

a handful of mini marshmallows

Serves 2

toast basics

Making toast couldn't be simpler, and it's usually the toppings that require a little more thought—sweet or savory, big or small, quick or leisurely, fat or thin? However, there are a few different techniques for making toast—all of them delicious, but each one a little bit different and creating a unique taste and texture. Crostini, brushed with oil and broiled, are explosively crisp, while sautéed French toast is deliciously, meltingly buttery. And toast is just toast—but utterly divine.

toast

4 slices of bread

Serves 2

Put the bread in a toaster and cook until golden brown. Alternatively, preheat the broiler, then toast the bread on one side until golden and flip over and cook the second side in the same way. Spread with butter, or the topping of your choice.

Note Watch your toast carefully because burnt toast just doesn't taste good. Different types of bread take different lengths of time to cook, so even if your toaster is set to cook perfect toast, a different type of bread can throw out the timings. If you burn it—just start again.

crostini

½ thin baguette

olive oil, for brushing

Serves 4

Slice the loaf into thin rounds and brush each one with olive oil. Press down onto a stovetop grill-pan, then cook for about 2 minutes until crisp and well marked, then flip over and cook the second side until brown. Alternatively, bake in a preheated oven at 375°F until crisp and golden. Add the topping of your choice.

bruschetta

4 slices of country-style sourdough bread

1 garlic clove, halved

olive oil, for sprinkling

Serves 4

Toast the bread on both sides until crisp and golden—in a toaster, under a preheated broiler, or on a stovetop grill-pan. Rub the cut side of the garlic over the toasts. Sprinkle with olive oil and serve immediately.

Note To make elegant, bitesize bruschetta, cut each slice of bread into 3 fingers before toasting.

french toast

2 eggs

2 tablespoons heavy cream

1 tablespoon butter

4 slices of white bread, brioche or challah

sea salt

maple syrup, to serve

Serves 2

Put the eggs, cream, and a pinch of salt in a bowl and beat briefly. Melt the butter in a nonstick skillet until sizzling, then dip the slices of bread in the egg mixture, and lay in the pan. Cook for about 2 minutes until golden, then flip over and cook for a further 2 minutes until golden. Serve with maple syrup.

index

conversion charts

Weights and measures have been rounded up or down slightly to make measuring easier.

Volume equivalents:

American	Metric	Imperial
1 teaspoon	5 ml	
1 tablespoon	15 ml	
¼ cup	60 ml	2 fl.oz.
⅓ cup	75 ml	2½ fl.oz.
½ cup	125 ml	4 fl.oz.
⅔ cup	150 ml	5 fl.oz. (¼ pint)
¾ cup	175 ml	6 fl.oz.
1 cup	250 ml	8 fl.oz.

Weight equivalents: Measurements:

Imperial	Metric	Inches	Cm
1 oz.	25 g	¼ inch	5 mm
2 oz.	50 g	½ inch	1 cm
3 oz.	75 g	¾ inch	1.5 cm
4 oz.	125 g	1 inch	2.5 cm
5 oz.	150 g	2 inches	5 cm
6 oz.	175 g	3 inches	7 cm
7 oz.	200 g	4 inches	10 cm
8 oz. (½ lb.)	250 g	5 inches	12 cm
9 oz.	275 g	6 inches	15 cm
10 oz.	300 g	7 inches	18 cm
11 oz.	325 g	8 inches	20 cm
12 oz.	375 g	9 inches	23 cm
13 oz.	400 g	10 inches	25 cm
14 oz.	425 g	11 inches	28 cm
15 oz.	475 g	12 inches	30 cm
16 oz. (1 lb.)	500 g		
2 lb.	1 kg		

Oven temperatures:

110°C	(225°F)	Gas ¼
120°C	(250°F)	Gas ½
140°C	(275°F)	Gas 1
150°C	(300°F)	Gas 2
160°C	(325°F)	Gas 3
180°C	(350°F)	Gas 4
190°C	(375°F)	Gas 5
200°C	(400°F)	Gas 6
220°C	(425°F)	Gas 7
230°C	(450°F)	Gas 8
240°C	(475°F)	Gas 9